THE BIG BOSS

Dear Ben you asked
me how I Knew there is
a God. Maybe this book will
give you some answers. It

Andy Robb

would be good if you asked
your dad where to find the
Stories it gives in this book.
Good Reading Love Grandad +N!
x x x o

The Big Boss

Copyright © 2005 John Hunt Publishing Ltd
The Bothy, Deershot Lodge, Park Lane, Ropley, Hants, SO24 0BE, UK
E-mail: office@johnhunt-publishing.com
www.johnhunt-publishing.com
www.o-books.net

Text: © 2005 Andy Robb
Illustrations © 2005 Andy Robb
Page layout by Andy Robb
Design by BookDesign™, UK

ISBN 1 842981 59 5

Scriptures quoted from the Good News Bible published by The Bible
Societies/HarperCollins Publishers Ltd., UK

A CIP catalogue record for this book is available from the British Library.

Printed in Singapore by TWP

CONTENTS

Have you ever wondered what God looks like?

Me too!

People have all sorts of **weird and wonderful** ideas about what they *think* God looks like.

In the movies God's portrayed as anything from an old man with a long white beard to an ordinary looking guy with a dapper white suit.

Sometimes people imagine God's a just mean old tyrant waiting to zap them with a **bolt of lightning** and other times they think God's little more than a **white cloud of nothingness** - all power and no personality.

But surprising as it seems, nobody actually really knows.

But at the Boring Bible we're not put off by that sort of thing, which is why in *this* book (*The Big Boss*) we're going all out to try and get ourselves our very own Boring Bible...

picture of God!

To find out what God is *actually* like (or maybe even *looks* like) we're gonna head for our best (and most reliable) source of info...**the Bible**! Chances are you've heard of this famous book once or twice (maybe you even *own* one).

But most people *don't* own one (let alone read it) which is why *you* need to know what's so special about this **worldwide bestseller**.

First off, the Bible is a book that's all about **God**.

Okay, so that might seem obvious to *many* of you but I don't want to be accused of being presumptious.

Not only that, but the Bible *also* fills you in with loads of info about stuff that God's *done*, like making the whole whopping big universe (including Planet Earth and everything on it), with stuff about what makes God tick, where God lives, what God thinks about you and me, how old God is, how big God is and whether God is a *good* God (or not).

So, that's the *Bible* for you.

If you *really* wanna get your teeth into all **66 books** of the Bible then a good way to get started is by getting your hands on a copy of Boring Bible book *Bible Buster* which will ease you in nice and gentle. How kind is that?

Let's move on.

The first bit of *The Big Boss* is all about some of the times that God decided to show up (big time) on Planet Earth.

Was God making a guest appearance a good thing?

Well, check out these brill bits from the Bible (we've just given you some edited highlights) and find out whether or not you'd *really* want to meet up with **The Big Boss**!

Are you sitting comfortably?...

...then I'll begin.

Cloud of Terror

If you've read Boring Bible *Magnificent Moses* then you'll know all about how God rescued the **Israelite** nation from the clutches of the rotten old Egyptian Pharaoh (using a little-used short cut through the Red Sea)...

...and how the Israelites ended up in the desert as they headed for a new home that God had lined up for them.

The whole story features in Bible book **Exodus**. ('Exodus' simply means a big group of people leaving a place - which is exactly what had just happened!).

'Cos the Israelites were a nation that God had handpicked to show the rest of the world what God was like (and what God expected from the *rest* of us) then *they* needed to be up to speed with exactly *how* God was planning to run his worldwide operation.

A team meeting with the Boss was now **top priority**!

The location for the meet-up with God was here...

Okay, so it's an *outdoor* meeting but an indoor venue for the team briefing with the Boss was *totally* out of the question. Trying to seat **two million** or so Israelites was gonna be a complete non-starter.

But meeting God wasn't just like turning up for a nine o'clock appointment.
God had a word with **Moses** (the guy in charge of the Israelites) and told them that they had two days to get themselves in tip-top condition for the meet-up.

That meant having a wash and brush-up but *also* making sure that they weren't doing things that their Boss disapproved of. God expected his team to be **spic and span** when he eventually showed up.

Oh, yes, one more itsy-bitsy thing.

No sneak previews of the meeting place!

In fact, here's how God put it...

> MARK A BOUNDARY ROUND THE MOUNTAIN THAT PEOPLE MUST NOT CROSS AND TELL THEM NOT TO GO UP THE MOUNTAIN OR EVEN GET NEAR IT. IF ANYONE SETS FOOT ON IT HE IS TO BE PUT TO DEATH.

No arguing with *that* then, is there?

Why was their Boss (God) being so strict?

It's because God is in a completely different *league* to human beings. The Bible says that God is so **holy** (that means he's not like us) that to waltz up to him casually is one **big mistake**.

So, a couple of days later, Moses marched all two million-ish Israelites up to the foot of the mountain and there they waited. Were the Israelites excited about meeting God?

Nope! They were **scared silly**!

God wasn't coming in by the back door for *this* mega-meeting with his chosen people - this was gonna be an entrance you couldn't miss (even if you wanted to).

First off, there was a **big, black thunder cloud** that dropped down onto the mountain (with a frightening display of **lightning** thrown in for free).

In case the Israelites *hadn't* noticed that God had arrived, a loud trumpet blast (from heaven) just about knocked them off their feet.

Worse was still to come.

'Fraid not. The *next* thing to happen was that the whole of Mount Sinai was covered with **thick smoke**. God had turned up in a fiery display of his power.

This wasn't the sort of cosy meeting with their Boss the Israelites had bargained on.

To add insult to injury, the noise of the trumpet kept getting louder and louder.

The Israelites were frightened out their pants.

And then God spoke so that everyone could hear.

Was it a soft, soothing voice?

No way! The Bible says that God's voice was like **thunder**.

The Israelites could stand it no more. They edged further and further away from the foot of the mountain. There was absolutely no way that *they* were gonna go up that mountain to meet up with their Boss - even *if* he gave them permission.

As it was, Moses and a bunch of leaders eventually went up in their place.

And guess what? They all lived to tell the tale.

In fact, the Bible handily tells us that when Moses *did* eventually return from his one-to-one with God his face was **shining**. Something of God's glory had rubbed off in him.

Just think what those Israelites missed out on.
If only they'd twigged that their Boss *wasn't* going to wipe them off the face of Planet Earth - he only wanted to make sure that they understood how **holy** he actually *was*.

Blazing Bush

Moses was a fella who was no stranger to meeting God.
His *first* encounter with The Big Boss was when he was on the
run from the Egyptians. (He'd killed one of them).
Moses had ended up in the middle of nowhere, looking after his
father-in-law's sheep and goats. It was far cry from his days as a
member of the **Egyptian royal family** (but that's *another* story).

You said it!
Anyway, Moses was out and about in the desert doing his stuff
as a shepherd (and *goatherd* or whatever someone's called who
looks after goats!) when something rather unusual caught his
eye...

Er, no that's not *quite* what I had in mind.

What I *meant* is that Moses had noticed that there was a bush on fire, nearby, but of all the strange things it didn't seem to be burning up.

Being an inquisitive sort of chap, Moses decided to take a closer look.

One thing Moses was probably *not* expecting was for the bush to answer back...

What do you say to a bush that knows your name?

I suppose the only thing is to keep the conversation going and just see what happens - which is *precisely* what Moses did.

As you've no doubt guessed by now, this was no ordinary bush. Well, okay, the *bush* was ordinary but what was *happening* to the bush *wasn't*.

God had decided to use this unconventional method to speak to Moses and it most *definitely* grabbed his attention.

God had more to say...

The Bible says that Moses covered his face. This was not your average glow that you'd get from a bonfire.

This was **God-powered illumination** and probably more than a top-of-the-range pair of shades could even cope with.

And as if Moses didn't have *enough* to do making sure he didn't get blinded he *also* suddenly had a severe attack of the **collywobbles.**

Moses was *well* afraid. God showing up had really shaken our main man. Just to fill you in with the *rest* of the story. God went on to tell Moses that he was planning a big escape plan for the Israelites who were slaves in Egypt. God might have *looked* awesome but he was still a kind God. That *hadn't* changed.

But I think we're getting the picture that God has gotta be taken a lot more seriously than most people think.

Time-out at the Temple

Just one last quick story from the Bible to give you an idea what it was like when God showed up on Planet Earth (but I think you're getting the picture already that you don't mess around with The Big Boss).

A bit of background to what's about to happen.

One of Israel's kings (**Solomon** - you've probably heard of him. He had 700 wives, yep, I'm serious) had built a very special building (**the Temple**) in Israel's capital city (**Jerusalem**) in which he was going to keep something called the **Ark of the Covenant**. No, this *wasn't* a boat like Noah's ark, this was an ornate box in which the Israelites stored one or two unusual mementoes of some of the miraculous things God had done for their nation.

The **Ark of the Covenant** was a sort of symbol that God (their Boss) was with them. Actually, it was a bit more than just a symbol 'cos God's power clung to that box wherever it went. Solomon and the Israelites believed that if the Ark of the Covenant was in the Temple... then so was God. Were they right? Let's check out what happened next.

Because this box was a bit special, it couldn't be lugged around by any old Tom, Dick or Harry...

The job of carrying the Ark had been assigned to a bunch of Israelites called **priests**. If anyone *else* laid a finger on it then it was curtains for them.

Anyway, back to the story.

So, with the priests carrying it, the Ark of the Covenant was taken to the Temple.

The Israelites were right to handle the box (and God) with care because the instant the priests headed for the exit, the place was filled with a **cloud shining with dazzling light**.

God had turned up again in all his power and glory.

The priests took the rest of the day off because there was absolutely no *way* they could carry on doing all their priestly stuff with God's presence filling the Temple.

Just *entering* the building again would have had them flat on their faces.

God's power would have knocked them for six, that's for sure!

Okay, so that's some stuff about God to get us up and running but it's not the *whole* story by any means.
Time to do a name check.

God hasn't just *one* name, like most people (okay, so some of you have got two or three names plus your surname thrown in for good measure).
But what we're talking about *here* is heaps and *heaps* of names which all tell you something about who God is, what God does and what God is like.

SO WHAT! MY NAME'S MABEL MEANING 'LOVEABLE' WHICH IS OBVIOUSLY WHAT I'M LIKE!

Fascinating Facts:

The Reverend Ralph William Lionel Tollemache (born 1826) had 12 kids who shared 100 different names between them!
The world's shortest name is simply any single letter of the alphabet, famously used by America's President Harry S Truman.
The most hesitant name recorded was used by three men in the Bible who were all called...Er!

NAMES IN A NUTSHELL

The Israelites had their very own name for God...

... which without any vowels was a bit of a mouthful so they made it into **YAHWEH**, which was pronounced ...

...which is *much* easier to say.

If you were wondering what YAHWEH (or Jehovah or even LORD as it's sometimes translated) means...

...then let me tell you.
It means '**the one who exists eternally** (forever)'.

Someone (not me, I've got better things to do) has worked out that there *could* be as many as **1,000** *different* names for God in the Bible.

So sometimes God was called...

Yahweh Jireh which means 'The Lord will provide'- showing that God is a God who wants to give us good things

Or even...
Yahweh Nissi which means 'The Lord is my Banner' - showing us that God is a God who fights for his people.

Or maybe...
Yahweh Shalom which means 'The Lord is Peace' - showing us that God is a God who wants to give us rest and peace inside.

Or then again...
Yahweh Sabbaoth which means 'The Lord of Hosts' - showing us that God can be portayed as military figure who commands all the armies of heaven.

Or perhaps...
Yahweh Ro'i which means 'The Lord my Shepherd' - showing us that God is a God who cares for us (just like a shepherd cares for the sheep of his pasture).

For your info there's one name that God's *never* called in the Bible and that's '**The Big Boss**'.

The only reason this Boring Bible book goes by *that* name is because if we'd gone and called it something like '**Yahweh Sabbaoth**' then none of you would ever have bought a copy let alone had a clue what it meant.

With the odd exception!

But at least calling it '**The Big Boss**' gives you an idea that God is bigger than us, more powerful than us...and that God's in charge of the whole show (running the universe).

Which leads us quite nicely on to...

Stuff God's Made

God isn't the sort of God who *just* likes to go around showing us how big and powerful he is all the time. God's *also* a dab hand at making things, or should I say *creating* things.

Let me show you what I mean by that.

The chances are you've probably done the odd bit of clay modelling (or play dough modelling) before.

It's great fun trying to make something artistic out of a bit of ordinary clay. But here's a question for you.

How would you get on if you *didn't* have a lump of **squidgy clay** to work with?

You wouldn't be able to make *anything*, would you?

Now listen up! The Bible tells us that it was God (the same God that we've been talking about all along) who created the whole vast universe that we live in.

But God didn't pop down to the corner store to *buy* all the stuff he needed to make stars and planets. God made them out of *nothing*, which is another way of saying that God *created* them. When *we* make anything we're only using the raw materials that *God* has already created.

Right, so the cats out of the bag - it was **God** who got the universe up and running.

Now, there's loads of different ideas doing the rounds about how the universe (stars, planets, earth, people) came into being, And *some* of them are as old as the hills or should I say *mountains*? The **ancient Greeks** (no that's not the elderly ones - it's Greeks who lived a long time ago, so don't try and be smart) believed that their gods on **Mount Olympus** caused everything in the world to happen. But sorry all you ancient Greeks, we're going to run with the *Bible's* take on things.

Yep! 'Cos we figure that the *best* person to tell us how it was at the very beginning of time would be someone who's been around a long time - longer than you or I - in fact, someone who was actually there when the whole thing got kick-started.

Not ancient enough, I'm afraid.
But *God* is.

Fascinating Fact:

*Did you know that God actually has a name
that tells us he's been around from the
very beginning of things?.
In Bible book Daniel, chapter 7 and verse 9
(if you're in a looking-up type mood)
God is described as the 'Ancient of Days' or
that he's been living for ever.*

Now, if you've suddenly got into one of those 'if God was there
at the start, then who made God?' ways of thinking then
I suggest that, for your own sanity, you snap right out of it this
instant!

Trying to work out
that sort of thing is
gonna **blow your
brains** and that's
not something
I wanna be around
to see.

You'll just have to take my word for it that what the Bible *says* is
true. There are *some* things that our human minds just can't get
a handle on and that's the end of it.

Another one of those things that's almost *guaranteed* to **boggle
your brain** is that God actually *made* time.

No that doesn't mean God makes watches and clocks but it
means that before God made the universe that we live in, God
first of all had to give it a **beginning**.

Flip the page and I'll try and explain...

If you're into **athletics** then you'll know all about racing down a running track. But before the starter gives you the cue to go, it's extremely important that there's a running track laid out in front of you for you to run on.

Just like your *running track* is gonna need a **start** and a **finish**, well so did God's *universe*!

Why's that? 'Cos God doesn't live in **time**. Where *God* lives there *isn't* any time. There's no start and there's no finish. The Bible says that God's *always* been around (and so's the place where God lives).

Yes I know that I'm about to set your brain on **primed-for-destruction** mode again but that's just the way it is!

Just stick with it, okay, we're nearly through the worst of this **brain-busting** bit.

So, when God wanted to create the *universe*, he *also* needed to create *time*.

Before God gave the command to the universe, "On your marks, get set, go!" God made a track for it all to run on (which was called '**time**') - time had a **start** and (eventually) a **finish**.

Everything that ever happened in God's universe from then on would happen at some point along the **line** (or track) of **time** that God had created.

And where is God in all this time stuff?

Well, God has a grandstand seat and can watch the whole thing from beginning to end.

Where God is...

Where we are...

I suppose that's why the Bible has so much stuff in it that predicts what is going to happen in the future - 'cos God can see it all from the **outside** looking **in**.

He can see the **beginning**...and he can see the **end**.

Now wouldn't *you* like to do that?

Anyway, let's get back to the business of God creating everything.

PHEW! THANK GOODNESS FOR THAT!

The big question is *how* did God create the stars, planets, animals and plants?

The simple answer is that God *told* it to happen - and it *did*!

Yep, it sure is! I'm sure God designed and planned it *first* but a word of command was all that was needed to bring it to life.

For the **full** facts on this one you'll do well to read it up in Boring Bible book *Ballistic Beginnings* but for now, at least you've got a bit of an idea what an amazing (and awesomely powerful) God he must be to be able to do stuff like that.

Did You Know?

The Bible actually answers that very question which many of us have asked. It says (in Bible book Romans, chapter 1 and verse 20) that...'Ever since God created the world, his invisible qualities, both his eternal power and divine nature, have been clearly seen; they are perceived in the things that God has made".

That simply means we can see what God is like (and that he exists) by looking at the things God's made.

In fact, let's check out some of...

God's Amazing Creations

First off, let's *look* into *eyes*. (Look? Eyes? Get it? Just my little joke!)

A very little joke - the Editor

Eyes are one of those things we all take for granted unless we maybe start to lose our sight and then we begin to appreciate what brilliant things eyes really are.

Did you know that each eye is made up of **137 million** special cells (give or take the odd one or two) which are called rods and cones. As light enters our eyes through the lens it falls on these cells and is then changed into electric signals which whiz along the optic nerve (at **300 miles an hour**) to our brain. Our brain is cram-packed with millions of electrical connections which turn these signals into pictures. But on top of that, our eyes can focus, they can see colour *and* they can take in moving images (like video cameras).

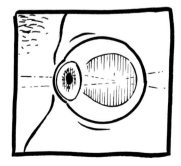

All in all, it looks like our eyes have been designed by a brilliant **creator God**, doesn't it?

Camouflage is one of God's fascinating inventions.
You've probably seen pictures of creatures like the **chameleon**
which changes colour to blend into the background or

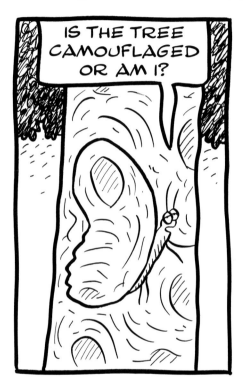

IS THE TREE CAMOUFLAGED OR AM I?

butterflies which have tree bark patterns on their wings to make them almost invisible when they are resting against the trunk of a tree.

Many creatures spend a lot of their time trying to make sure that they don't get **munched for lunch** by another *bigger* creature and having the ability to disguise itself is at least *one* way of giving it a fighting chance of survival.

There's no *way* that these creatures could have come up with the idea of camouflage themselves 'cos camouflage only works when it's seen from a distance - and there's no way that these cleverly-disguised creatures could do *that*, is there?

What's needed is someone to design their camouflage *for* them.
Someone like a **creator God**.

Animated Oats (yes I'm serious) are *another* one of God's weird and wonderful ideas.

You thought that animals (and people) were the only ones to get about by walking. Well think again!

Meet the Animated Oat...

This unusual seed (from North Africa) 'walks' along the ground. As you probably know, all plants need to distribute their seeds (another of God's brill ideas) so that *more* plants can grow. The Animated Oat seed has long whiskers (called '**awns**') and when it falls from the plant, the moisture in the air makes the seeds **twist and turn** along the ground, giving it the appearance of walking.

This is the seed's way of making sure it gets far enough away from the parent plant (don't you try this with *your* parents!) then, using the awns as levers, it pulls itself into the soil and anchors itself there ready to grow *another* oat plant.

Yet *another* masterpiece of design from...yes, you guessed it.

A creator God!

Hope you found that interesting.

In a bit we're gonna tell you something you've no doubt been itching to know...**where God lives** (and I don't mean in a house). We're talking God's actual *address* here.

(Yes, we *did* take a look at a Bible bit that had some stuff about God taking up residence in the Temple but that was really God's Spirit - God never actually left where the he was living. Sounds a little mystifying doesn't it? But don't forget that God (unlike us) has the ability to be *everywhere*...all at the same time!

Before your mind gets even *more* bamboozled, we'll just leave it at that, shall we?

From what we've checked out so far you could be forgiven for thinking that God is so **big and powerful** that you couldn't get within fifty zillion miles of him without being reduced to a lump of **quivering jelly**...

But the good news is that that's not the end of it.
There's much more to God where *that* came from.
At the Boring Bible we're gonna try and give you the *whole* picture.

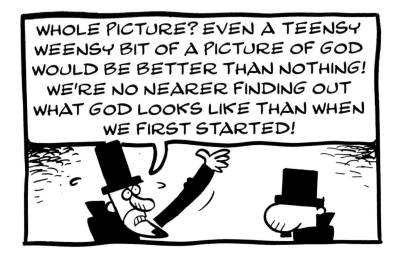

To discover some *more* brill stuff about God you're gonna need your very own **Boring Bible Codecracker**....

If you've read Boring Bible book *Saints Alive!* then you'll know how this state of the art, cunningly clever piece of codecracking equipment works.

(Alright, so maybe we're exaggerating its benefits just a little, but it is *quite* good, honest!)

If I set you a code like *this*,..

YLIRMT

...all you've gotta do is look along the **Codecracker** to find white code letter '**Y**' and to see what letter is above it which in this case is the letter '**B**'. *Next* up is white code letter '**L**' which is below the a '**O**' and so on until you've decoded the word '**BORING**'.

Happy codecracking!

TLW RH UZRGSUFO

Bible book 1 Corinthians chapter 1 and verse 9

Wasn't too hard was it?
Next one up is...

ML LMV RH TLLW

VCXVKG TLW ZOLMV

Bible book Luke chapter 18 and verse 19

And now...

YV KVIUVXG QFHG ZH BLFI UZGSVI

RM SVZEVM RH KVIUVXG

Bible book Matthew chapter 5 and verse 48

And here's a whopper to get your teeth into...

BLF ZIV Z TLW DSL ULITREVH

BLF ZIV TIZXRLFH ZMW OLERMT

HOLD GL YV ZMTIB

BLFI NVIXB RH TIVZG

Bible book Nehemiah chapter 9 and verse 17

Nearly finished...

TLW WLVH MLG

XSZMTV

Bible book James chapter 1 and verse 17

And last, but not least...

TLW RH ORTSG ZMW RM

SRN GSVIV RH ML WZIPMVHH

ZG ZOO

Bible book 1 John chapter 1 and verse 5

Well, there you have it - well I *hope* you have.
If you got stuck on any of them, here are the answers in the
order they appeared - but *only* as a last resort. That's why we've
flipped them!

GOD IS LIGHT AND IN HIM THERE IS NO DARKNESS AT ALL.

GOD DOES NOT CHANGE.

YOU ARE A GOD WHO FORGIVES. YOU ARE GRACIOUS AND LOVING. SLOW TO BE ANGRY. YOUR MERCY IS GREAT.

BE PERFECT JUST AS YOUR FATHER IN HEAVEN IS PERFECT.

NO ONE IS GOOD EXCEPT GOD ALONE.

GOD IS FAITHFUL.

I don't know if you picked it up, but *one* of those Codecrackers didn't actually call God '**God**' - it called him '**Father**'.

Why did it call God *Father*? Here's why.

So far, when we've talked about God, it's as if we've talking about just *one* person, which is fair enough.

But here's where things start to get a bit **brain-stretching** again.

Although the Bible talks about there being **one God**, he's actually made up of **three people**.

Now whatever you do, don't lose me at this point.

Because we're not God (we're people - if you hadn't noticed) then trying to figure out God-type things is sometimes just about **impossible**.

And, wait for it...*this* is one of those times!

Here's what the Bible says.

The Bible says that God is...

a) Father

That God is...

b) Son (Jesus Christ)

And that God is...

c) Holy Spirit.

Boring Bible Info:

If you want to impress an adult (unless you happen to be an adult already who's sneakily reading this book while nobody's looking!) then tell them that you've just learned all about the **Godhead**. (That's just a fancy way of saying that Father, Son and Holy Spirit are all God, all equal and all work together as God).

By the way, just for your info, if you ever hear someone talking about the **Trinity** then they're talking about the same thing as the Godhead.

With that, I think we'll leave this tricky bit...

...'cos there are *some* things about God that are just too **mind-bongling** for us to *ever* get our human minds around.

The plus side of all this means that God isn't like us.

I don't think *any* of us would want a God running the universe who was just like you and me, would we?

Right, the moment you've all been waiting for...

Er, sorry, not quite!

What I *meant* is that after a bit of a build up we're *finally* gonna tell you...**where God lives**.

The Boring Bible

NOT

TOP SECRET DEPT!

After a thorough and detailed investigation, requiring thousands of man hours, using the very latest research technology, we, at the Boring Bible, have finally discovered where, exactly, God lives.

(Well, actually I'm exaggerating a bit. In fact I just looked it up in the **Bible**, but I figured that a bit of a big build-up would grab your interest more!)

So, here it is...**God's address**.

Yep, just '**heaven**'!
To be blunt about it, God doesn't usually take visitors much anyway. Most people who pop in to heaven generally don't have a return ticket - but that's *another* story.

So there you have it. **God's address**.
But the question you're probably asking *now* is...

Hmm! Not such an easy peasy one to answer I'm afraid.
Put it like this.
Remember that stuff we said about God being outside time
earlier on?

Well, **heaven** is a place that you won't be able to see until you actually *get* there (and if you wanna be *sure* of taking up permanent residence in heaven once you've finished with Planet Earth then check out Boring Bible book *Crazy Christians* for the full booking details).

Because God isn't flesh and bones like you and me (he's **spirit** if you must know) that means the place where God lives has gotta be the same sort of thing (spirit).

But that doesn't stop God getting stuck into things down here. God's actively involved in keeping the universe ticking over but - and here's the clever bit - God can do it without leaving heaven. His spirit (as we've already said) is *everywhere* which means that *God* is everywhere.

And if you're in the mood for another fancy word how about road testing this one...'**Omnipresent**'.

Okay, that's enough of the road testing.
Omnipresent means '**God is everywhere**' (as we've just said).

Fascinating Fact:

*Not only is God Omnipresent (God's everywhere),
not only is God Omnipotent (God has unlimited power)
but God is also
Omniscient which means
that God knows everything!*

I think we're drifting a bit.

Back to checking out about where God lives.

So we've established that we're *not* gonna get a sneak preview of heaven until we **pop our clogs** (die) but the *good* news is that the Bible is quite up front about what heaven's like and what goes on there so I reckon that a bit of *secondhand* info is better than *none*.

Let's have a look and see what we can find out...

What is heaven like?

Our *first* port of call, for a brill description of God's home, is from Bible book **Revelation** (the very last book in the Bible, if you're interested)...

...chapter 4 and verses 2 through to 11.

THUNDER THRONE!

'There in heaven was a throne with someone sitting on it. His face gleamed like such precious stones as jasper and carnelian and all round the throne was a rainbow the colour of emerald. In a circle round the throne were twenty-four other thrones on which were seated twenty-four elders dressed in white and wearing crowns of gold.
From the throne came flashes of lightning...

...rumblings and peals of thunder.

In front of the throne seven lighted torches were burning, which are the seven spirits of God.

Also in front of the throne there was what looked like a sea of glass, clear as crystal...

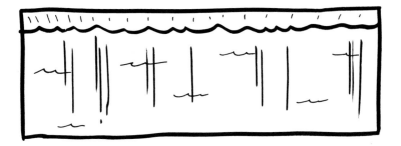

Surrounding the throne on each of its sides were four living creatures covered with eyes in front and behind.

The first one looked like a lion, the second looked like a bull, the third had a face like a man's face and the fourth looked like an eagle in flight.

Each one of the four living creature had six wings and they were covered with eyes, inside and out.

Day and night they never stopped singing...

The four living creatures sing songs of glory and honour and thanks to the one who sits on the throne, who lives for ever and ever.

When they do so, the twenty-four elders fall down before the thrown and worship him whom lives for ever and ever.

They throw their crowns down in front of the throne and say...'

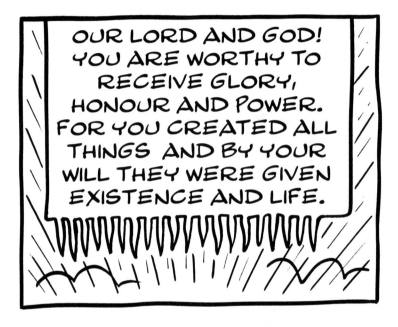

OUR LORD AND GOD! YOU ARE WORTHY TO RECEIVE GLORY, HONOUR AND POWER. FOR YOU CREATED ALL THINGS AND BY YOUR WILL THEY WERE GIVEN EXISTENCE AND LIFE.

A chunk from Bible book Revelation, chapter 4, verses 2 to 11

So, as you can see, heaven isn't people floating round on fluffy white clouds, playing nice little harps and getting bored out of their brains at the thought of having to do that for ever and ever.

Next up, *another* awesome snapshot of what **God's HQ** is like...

HOLY SMOKE!

'In the year that King Uzziah died, I saw the Lord. He was sitting on his throne, high and exalted, and his robe filled the whole Temple.

Round him flaming creatures were standing, each of which had six wings.

Each creature covered its face with two wings and its body with two and used the other two for flying.

They were calling out to each other...

The sound of their voices made the foundation of the Temple shake and the Temple itself was filled with smoke.'

A chunk from Bible book Isaiah, chapter 6, verses 1 to 4

When you see how those creatures talk about God, it makes you realise that using God's name carelessly (like as a swear word) is a mega big **no-no**!

Did You Know?

Although God is all-powerful, God's knows everything and God's everywhere, he still doesn't run the show single-handed.

God's got a whole *team* working for him, not only in heaven but also down here on Planet Earth. The guys that do the *most* to-ing and fro-ing are **God's angels**. They're the awesome beings who can show up *here* but can also still be in God's *presence* at one and the same time. Don't ask me *how* they do it - they just *do*. Sometimes, when angels put in a sudden appearance, it's so awesome that people think they've actually seen God himself. Which leads me nicely on to our *next* bit where we're gonna take a crash course in what to do (and what *not* do) were you to **meet God** (or perhaps even one of his angels for that matter). Meeting someone mega important can be a bit of an ordeal especially if it's someone like a **President** or a **Queen**.

So, if you're gonna have a **face to face** meeting with **God** then it's even *more* important that you know the rights and wrongs of how you should behave.

To save you any awkwardness and embarrassment (should such an opportunity arise) we're gonna take a look at some people (in the Bible) who got it **right** - and some who got it **wrong**.

Adam and Eve...get it wrong!

Adam and Eve (the world's first two people) had the run of Planet Earth, which included a rather splendid garden (**the Garden of Eden**) which they were basically in charge of. Just one itty bitty rule. No touching the tree which gives knowledge of what is good and what is bad.

Unfortunately for Adam and Eve, God's enemy (the devil) was aware of this minor restriction and he set about a cunning plan to get the pair to **fall foul of God**.

Just so's Adam and Eve didn't *suspect* anything, the devil slithered into the Garden in the guise of a serpent. Sneaky!

Very unwisely, Adam and Eve disobeyed God and chomped away on the forbidden fruit.

When God showed up later in the day, did they put out the red carpet for their creator God?

Nope, they hid. But not for long. God found them.

That's because God is...yes, you've got it...**omnipresent**. God's everywhere so *hiding* from God and trying to *cover up* something you've done wrong isn't gonna cut much ice with him. That's the *wrong* way to meet up with God. And because God *knows* everything...

HE'S OMNISCIENT!

...correct, then the best thing you can do is **come clean** and tell him you're **sorry** and you won't do it again.

Abraham...gets it right!

Abraham (previously known as Abram, but that's another story - check out Boring Bible book *Hotchpotch Hebrews*) was sitting outside his tent (well, in the porch actually) trying his level best to avoid getting sunburn...

THE SOONER SOMEBODY INVENTS SUN LOTION THE BETTER!

...when he had a surprise visit from three men.

Did Abraham wait for the unexpected visitors to introduce themselves?

No way! Our main man hot-footed it (as fast as his elderly legs could carry him) to where the men were and fell face down on the dusty ground in front of them.

Next up, Abraham got his wife to rustle up a tasty meal for the honoured guests.

Abraham was totally on the ball with what he'd done (including getting a face-full of dirt).

Just round the corner in this Bible bit it's revealed that *two* of the visitors were in fact **angels** and the other one was **God** himself (or **LORD**, as the Bible puts it).

Abraham not only sensed that there was something special about these visitors but he also did the **right thing**.

Good on you Abraham!

Uzzah...gets it wrong!

We've already featured the **Ark of the Covenant** in *The Big Boss* but here's a Bible story that shows how *careful* you've gotta be when you're dealing with God.

A guy called **David**...

...was the king of Israel and he was keen to bring the Ark of the Covenant back to **Jerusalem** (Israel's capital city). As we've said before, this rather special box represented God's presence with the Israelites, so there was no time to waste in returning it to its rightful home in Jerusalem's **Temple**.

But in his haste, King David forgot that when you're dealing with God, there's a *right* way...and there's a *wrong* way!

On this particular day, King David chose the *wrong* way.

If David had only taken a bit of time to do a spot of research then he would have found out that God had given detailed instructions on how (and how *not*) to carry the Ark of the Covenant.

First off, the the only people allowed by God to carry the box were **Levites** (Israelite men appointed by God to serve him).

And secondly, there were hoops on the side of the Ark through which carrying poles were to be put.

But guess how David had the box carried?

I'll tell you. On an **ox-drawn cart**!

As the Ark of the Covenant made its journey back to Jerusalem, the oxen stumbled and a guy called **Uzzah** reached out to grab the box to stop it falling off.

Big mistake 'cos it cost Uzzah his life.

God killed him right where he stood because he didn't show the slightest bit of **reverence for God** (which means that he didn't show God any respect).

Treating God **casually** is definitely the *wrong* thing to do but on the *plus* side, a bit later on, King David tried a *second* time to bring the Ark of the Covenant back to Jerusalem - and *this* time he did it *God's* way.

Mary...gets it right!

If you've been paying attention then you'll have picked up the fact that **Jesus is God**.

What we're gonna drop in on now is a Bible story where somebody recognises **Jesus** for who he is (**God**).

That might sound a strange thing to say but not *everyone* thought (or thinks) that Jesus was anything more than just a good man.

For the *full* details about Jesus's life you're gonna need to part company with your hard-earned cash and fork out for a copy of the highly recommended Boring Bible book *Super Son* (highly recommended by *me*, that is!)

We pick up the story about a week before Jesus is executed and Jesus is visiting some friends (Mary, Martha and Lazarus).

Lazarus was a guy Jesus had miraculously brought back to life after he'd been dead in a tomb a for a few days.

Anyway, sticking to the story, not only was *Jesus* in the house but so were Jesus's *disciples* (the team he'd trained up to carry on doing God-type stuff after he'd died and returned to heaven).

Mary took everyone by surprise by pouring a mega big bottle of **expensive perfume** over Jesus's feet and then proceeded to wipe it off with her long hair.

It was Mary's way of showing how special she thought Jesus was but not *everyone* was quite so upbeat about the whole thing.

Judas (the disciple who cashed in his friendship with Jesus for thirty pieces of silver and then betrayed Jesus into the hands of his enemies) thought that it was a complete waste of money. But Judas had completely missed the point.

What Mary did was *her* way of **worshipping Jesus as God**. So *worshipping* God is the *right* way to approach God.

The Babylonians...get it wrong!

We're gonna head right back to the early years of the world's history to discover that you can't outsmart God.

Just to set the scene, this is after the flood that wiped most people (the wicked ones, that is) off the face of the Planet Earth. **Noah** (the guy with the ark) and Noah's family were the only survivors (because Noah was a man who tried to live his life in a way that pleased God).

God had given Noah (and his family) strict instructions to have loads of kids and repopulate the world.

All seemed to be going to plan until (many years later) Noah's descendants decided that they'd gone far enough, thank you very much and downed luggage at a place called **Babylonia** (or Shinar as it's *also* called).

Not wanting to waste any time in making their mark on the Babylonian landscape, these new settlers set about working together to build a **whopping great tower**.

Nothing wrong with that you may think - but that's where you'd be wrong.

No, what I mean is that *firstly*, they'd disobeyed God and decided *not* to keep on moving so that the whole world could be repopulated.

And *secondly*, they were now getting round to thinking that they could live quite happily *without* God, thank you very much!

This whole tower thing was *their* way of making out that they were on a level with God. These settlers were beginning to get a bit too big for their boots.

The plan was to build the tower so that it reached right up to heaven.

In actual fact, it wouldn't be much different in size (and shape) to a pyramid so it was hardly gonna get them *that* far (not that you could really get to heaven even if you made a tower a zillion miles high). But these settlers didn't have a route map to heaven so a tower was their best shot.

Now here's the funny bit.

The Bible says that while these settlers were busily trying to make a bit of a name for themselves by getting *up* to heaven... God came *down*.

To add insult to injury, God then went and mixed up their language so instead of there being just the *one* language, there were now *loads* of languages.

Now that they couldn't all communicate with each other the stubborn settlers had to no choice but to move on to other lands (with just the people who spoke *their* particular language).

Nice move!

So, setting yourself up against God (as if you don't *need* him or as if you're on the *level* with him) is *not* a good thing!

Saul...gets it right!

The *last* person we're gonna examine is a guy called **Saul**.
Saul didn't have any time for **Christians** (that's peope who
follow Jesus), in fact he hated Christians with a vengence
and would stop at *nothing* to make life a misery for them.
Saul even went so far as getting them arrested on trumped-up
charges, knowing full well that there was a good chance they'd
be executed.

All *that* was about to change.
Saul was headed for a place called **Damascus** so that he could
arrest any Christians he could lay his scheming hands on.
What Saul *hadn't* bargained on was what happened next.

As Saul approached the city of Damascus, he was suddenly stopped in his tracks by the **brightest light** he'd ever seen. The dazzling light flashed all round him and Saul fell to the ground.

From nowhere a voice said...

This bit from the Bible happened after Jesus had died, had come back to life again and had then gone back to heaven.

But Jesus most definitely *wasn't* going to put up with the stuff that Saul was doing to the Christians who were still carrying on his work on Planet Earth.

So Jesus had stepped in and called a halt to Saul's dirty tricks.

How did Saul take to meeting up with Jesus (God)?

I'll have you know that he was a **changed man**.

Saul threw in the towel and packed up persecuting Christians. Not only that...Saul become a Christian *himself*!

Saul realised that to fight *against* God (The Big Boss) is one **big mistake**.

And just to prove the point that he was a changed man, Saul also changed his name to **Paul**.

Saul (or should I say, *Paul*) *certainly* got it right when he met up with God.

Being really kind and helpful at Boring Bible HQ we thought you'd find it really helpful if we showed you how God the Father, Jesus the Son and the Holy Spirit all work together as a **slick operation**.

THE ACTION TEAM!

If you've been on your toes as you've read this book...

...you'll have picked up that early on in history (like at the very beginning) people and God fell out **big time**.

I have to tell you that it was rather **one-sided**.

As far as God was concerned, all *God* wanted was for human beings to enjoy being the **apple of his eye**.

But **Adam and Eve** (the first two human beings) had their eyes on an **apple** of their own (well, it wasn't an apple at all, actually - it was an unnamed fruit...

...but an apple makes a better play on words, doesn't it?).

The long and the short of it was that **Adam and Eve** ended up eating the fruit that God had said was completely out of bounds...

...and the pair immediately lost their innocence - just like God knew would happen. That's *why* God had urged them *not* to. From then on in, human beings and God lived separate lives. Okay, so occasionally someone would come along who'd remember that there was a God up there, somewhere, but by and large, people got on with their rather selfish (and God-less) lives and God...well, what *did* God do?

Well, one things for sure, although the human race was ignoring *God* - God was not ignoring *them*. God had the world and it's inhabitants very much still **in his sights**.

The Action Team in heaven (otherwise known as the Godhead)
were planning something behind the scenes that was gonna take the world by storm.

Father (God) was dead set on getting his creation (people) back to being his friends. In fact, more than just friends.

God the Father wanted **children** - people who he could care for (like every good dad *does*).

That meant that somehow God was gonna have to turn things right round so that human beings not only knew *about* their creator (God) but they *knew* him intimately as their Father (in heaven).

This was the audacious **mission** that God was planning to pull off.

But now for the **downside**.

Even if people *wanted* to become children of God (and some did) there was no way they *could*.

All of that rotten old **sin** was getting in the way. Haven't we mentioned sin yet? Oops, sorry. Well read on and I'll fill you in!

For your info, **sin** is stuff that we do that God says we *shouldn't* do and stuff that we're *not* doing that God says we *should* be doing.
Got that?

Anyway, as I said, all of that **sin** was acting like some kind of whopping great big wall between people and God. And although people might have got used it it...

...God most definitely hadn't!

(And a very *long* 'Did You Know?' it is too!) Although the world's very first celebrity couple (**Adam and Eve**) blew it big time by disobeying God, they didn't actually *start* the whole thing off.

Not so fast! Adam and Eve were still guilty for their disobedience...

...but the person who was responsible (or should I say **irresponsible**?) for *enticing* them to be disobedient was none other than **God's No.1 enemy**, the devil.

Some people think the devil is just some made up character, but you only have to take a look at the mess that this world is in to see the result of his evil handiwork which got kick-started in the Garden of Eden.

As we've already said, it was the devil who cunningly persuaded Adam and Eve to eat the forbidden fruit in the first place. And why, you may ask, did the devil stoop so low as to drive a wedge between God and people?

Well, let me tell you.

Before God had got around to creating Planet Earth (and the universe in which it snugly sits) there was just **God**...and **heaven**.

But before you start to feel sorry for God and think he was all on his lonesome, let me tell you that heaven was a **hubbub of heavenly activity**.

There were all *sorts* of creatures and creations (and there still are) sharing the place with God.

Heaven was choc-a-block *full* of life and activity.

One of the *main* inhabitants of heaven were **God's angels** - those powerful guys who act as God's messengers to Planet Earth.

One of the top angels (if not the *toppest*) was the devil himself.

'Toppest'? What sort of word is that? If you don't brush up on your grammar pronto then we're going to have to answer to lots of irate parents! - *The Editor*

Grovel, grovel. My sincerest apologies Mr Editor sir.

Anyway, as I was saying, the devil, (so the Bible tells us) was a mega high up angel but in those days he went by the name of...

Lucifer.

Lucifer was beautiful and powerful and was one of God's most awesome creatures. But Lucifer made a **big mistake**.

He got a bit **too big for his boots** and set his sights on being the No.1 inhabitant of heaven.

Just one problem.

That was *God's* position.. and it wasn't up for grabs.

In fact, there was no *way* one of God's creations (however beautiful and powerful) was gonna weasle his way into the driving seat of heaven.

This was *God's* show so it was absolutely *essential* that God was running things.

There was only one course of action open to God.

God booted Lucifer out of heaven.

Lucifer's wicked plan to oust God from his throne had turned Lucifer bad - and there was definitely no room for even the *teensiest* bit of grot in whiter-than-white heaven.

Lucifer (now called the devil) ended up somewhere between heaven and earth.

And with the door of heaven firmly shut the devil set about trying to make a name for himself somewhere else...**Earth**! Not only that, but to make matters worse, he *also* began to hatch an evil plan to try and get his own back on God.

And, being the smarty pants readers that you are...

...you've probably already worked out that this evil plan involved **a piece of fruit** and a couple of people called **Adam and Eve**.

And as we all now know, *that* was when the rot set in, no thanks to God's No.1 enemy.

As I was saying a while back, the *good* news for us human beings is that God *hadn't* turned his back on his creation and most of the Bible is actually all about **God's amazing plan** to get us back to being his friends again.

Time for God (the **Father**) to fill in Jesus (the **Son**) with the plan.

Jesus was going to have to do the almost unthinkable.

The Father was going to ask Jesus to leave heaven (the place where Jesus had always lived) and to visit Planet Earth.

But this was no ordinary visit.

Jesus wasn't going to turn up in a powerful display of thunder and lightning. Jesus was gonna show up as...

...**a man**!

Well, perhaps a just *little* more manly than that.

But a man the world had never seen the like of before.
Jesus was going to be God *and* man **all wrapped up in one**!
And here's why.

God (the Father) couldn't let all of us humans off the hook for our sin - we needed to be **punished**.

Yep, but God's *also* fair and just.
I mean, how would *you* feel if your parents never punished you for doing wrong?

Okay, but supposing your brother or sister or a friend does something that upsets *you* and all your parents do is this...

My point *exactly*!

'Cos God's a fair and a good God he knows that wrongdoing (sin) has just gotta be punished.

Some Bad News and Some Good News!

The *bad* news is that the punishment for sinning against God (so the Bible quite handily informs us) is **death**.

But the *good* news is that Jesus (the Son) was being sent to Planet Earth by God (the Father) to take that punishment *for* us.

Yeah, I suppose it is.

I know, how about we get someone from Planet Earth to volunteer to take the punishment for everbody else's sin?

All we need is a **willing volunteer**.

You can rest easy 'cos *none* of you would be suitable.

Nor, for that matter, would *any* of us.

If you've read Boring Bible book *Magnicent Moses* then you'll know a little bit about the **animal sacrifices** that God told the Israelites to make.

The Israelites had to sacrifice **perfect animals** to God to cover over their sin and to make *peace* with God.

But *now* God was lining up a perfect sacrifice that wouldn't just cover *over* peoples' sin - it would get rid of it for *good*.

A sinless man was required - which ruled out the whole human race in one stroke.

That's where Jesus (the Son) comes in.

If a perfect God can somehow *also* become a human being then what you've got is **the man for the job**.

If you've had a look at Boring Bible books *Super Son* or *Crackers Christmas* then you'll know all the stuff about how Jesus became a human being.

Too right, but nothing *whatsoever* to do with a jolly, fat man in a silly red suit.

It gives you an idea of what a tight unit the **Action Team** are, that Jesus didn't even so much as *quibble* with the difficult mission that God the Father was sending him on.

Just to warn you, there are **four Bible books** given over to filling you in with all the info about Jesus's mission to Planet Earth but we've only got a few pages in which to cram the whole thing in. So, here's the choices...

a) we can either appeal to your superior intellect and sheer, unmatched brainy-ness by giving it to you as a nice big **wadge of words**.

b) or we can do it as a **cartoon strip type thingummybob**.

Er, right! In that case, I think we'll go for the cartoons.

Just before we get cracking with the cartoons I thought you'd like to know about our rather handy **Boring Bible Ridiculously-easy-to-use Action Team Spotting System** (BBRATSS®*)
In fact it's *so* simple to understand that even a single-cell *Amoeba* could comprehend it!

Right, so here's how **BBRATSS**®* works.

F Means **Father** God is involved with the action.

S Means Jesus the **Son** of God is part of the action.

H Means the **Holy** Spirit of God is getting stuck in.

*This doesn't actually mean we've registered the **BBRATSS** acronym - it just means that we've discovered where this nice little ® symbol *is* on our computer keyboard and we wanted an excuse for using it!

Now that that's all clear, here's the cartoon strip type thingummybob...

Have a think who the **dove** represented?
Clue: It wasn't the Father or the Son.

If you're wondering whether that was the *end* of the Action Team's work then nothing could be further from the truth.
In fact, it was just the *beginning*.
With the problem of nasty old **sin** done and dusted...

...the way was open for *everyone* to get back to being friends with God.
It was now up to **Jesus's disciples** to carry on doing the stuff that Jesus had started.

But how on earth were a bunch of **bog-standard Israelites** gonna do miracles, healings and teach with authority?

NOT FORGETTING RAISING THE DEAD!

Quite so! Well, if you remember a couple of pages back, didn't Jesus say something about his Father sending power?

The power he was talking about was the **Holy Spirit**.

God's brill plan was to send the Holy Spirit so he could live in the disciples so that *they* could do the mega stuff that *Jesus* had been doing.

Not only that but the offer was also gonna be available to *every* human being who accepted that Jesus had taken the rap for their sin.

So there you have it.

A brill example of the **Action Team**...in action.

God the **Father** sends his **Son** to get rid of sin.

People who buy into what he's done get their sins forgiven, get back to being friends with God (in fact God calls them his children) and then God comes to live inside of them as the **Holy Spirit** to make it all real and to help them live like they really *are* God's children.

Now that's what I *call* a successful mission for the Action Team!

Fascinating Fact:

Did you know that God knows how many hairs there are on your head? The Bible says that every hair we have (or had) is numbered, which is good to know 'cos sometimes we can think that the God who created the whole, vast universe isn't interested in little ol' me - but now you know the truth...God is!

While we're on the subject of how well God knows us, I'll let you in on *another* secret (well, it's not a secret *really*, it just sounds more interesting when I put it like that!).

Jesus wasn't the *only* one to have an open line to chat with his Father in heaven (praying to him).

We do as well.

You can forget your phone 'cos calls to God won't cost you a penny!

Okay, so what I'm about to say isn't anything new to loads of you but I'll bet *some* of you have never even so much as *thought* about having **a chat with the creator of the universe**.
Come to think of it, put like that, it sounds a bit awesome, doesn't it.
Here's how it works.

Hotline to Heaven

Before you dial up God, you'd better check out the '**do's**' and '**don'ts**' of your telephone manner.
First off, you need to know *who* can give God a call.
Can *anyone*?
The answer is **yes** and **no**.

Let me explain.
Supposing you decide to call a friend and ask them to do something for you.
Imagine if it went something like this...

Hardly the *best* way to talk to your mate, is it?

It's the same with talking to God.

First off, don't start telling God all the things you want from him. That's a *bad* attitude to have.

And you've gotta show God some respect. If you treated your best friend like that you wouldn't get very far and it's the same with God.

You've gotta treat God like he's special.

God's *not* like a vending machine where you shove in your money and out pops what you want.

Talking to God is a **two-way** thing.

God's got stuff he wants to say to *you* as well as stuff you wanna say to *him*, so **pin back your lugholes** and take time out to **listen**.

And make sure you get to know God a bit better before you start reeling off a list of what you want.

Chances are, the better you get to know God the more likely you are to start asking God for things that *he* wants you to have.

That way your prayers will stop being selfish (and just for the record, God never answers that kind of prayer *anyway*).

And last but not least, don't let's forget that's it's only 'cos Jesus gave up his life for you that you can have a direct line to God at all!

So, **yes**, anyone *can* chat to God.

But **no**, not *every* prayer will get an answer.

Only the sort of prayers that fit in with what's best for your life - the way that *God* sees it!

If there's one thing I reckon we've picked up from this book it's that God's really quite approachable...but you've gotta know the *right* way to approach him.

Makes sense doesn't it.

After all, like we said earlier on, you wouldn't just waltz up to some bigwig (like a president or a queen) without thinking twice about it.

Same thing with God.

Anyway, seeing as you've been such good a good and patient reader, I think you deserve a **nice little story**.

It's all about a fella called **Moses**.

He's the guy who gets a whole Boring Bible book to himself - *Magnificent Moses*.

Nice one Moses!

Moses Sees God (well sort of)!

Moses...

...had been given (by God) the rather unenviable job of leading the **Israelite** nation out of slavery and into a new land (**Canaan**) which God had promised them.

The plan was for the Israelites to *return* the compliment and to show their gratitude, by letting God have the **No.1 slot** in their lives.

As Moses was soon to discover, the Israelites were prone to be somewhat **stubborn**...

It was a real tougie heading up those **stiff-necked Israelites** and Moses was needing a bit of **TLC** (tender loving care) from God to make things better.

Moses had gone up on to **Mount Sinai** (where God's presence happened to be at that particular moment) to take some time out with God.

What the Israelites main man was after was a bit of reassurance from God that God was still with him and that he didn't have to do this leading-the-Israelites-business single-handed.

And a peek at God in all his splendour and majesty might *just* do the trick as far as our Moses was concerned.

Not being one to be backward in coming forward, *Moses* came straight to the point...

And here's what *God* had to say on the matter...

So Moses *did* get to see God - but only from *behind*.
Which is probably the nearest anyone's got to catching a
glimpse of the creator of the universe.
But then again most of us *wouldn't* want to risk losing our lives
out of simple curiosity just to see what God looks like, would
we?

Did You Know?

Try as they might, nobody has ever actually
seen God face to face.
People have seen displays of his power and
splendour and Bible book John chapter 1 and
verse 18 backs up what we're saying.

But here's the good news. If you are one of God's children then
when you eventually go to heaven (when you die) you're gonna
see your Father in heaven face to face, in all his glory.

Well, it looks like were headed for the end of *The Big Boss*.
Before we bid you a fond farewell...

...I figured that it would be good to give you a quick reminder
of some of the stuff that we've checked out about God.
Just to keep your interest up until the very last page...

...we've lined up a few more **Codecrackers** for you to decipher.
All of them are designed to jog your memory about what God's
like.
Off you go!

CODECRACKER

A	B	C	D	E	F	G	H	I	J	K	L	M	N
Z	Y	X	W	V	U	T	S	R	Q	P	O	N	M

O	P	Q	R	S	T	U	V	W	X	Y	Z
L	K	J	I	H	G	F	E	D	C	B	A

Here's your first one...

TLW RH XIVZGLI

Now try this...

TLW RH KVIUVXG

And this...

TLW RH OLERMT

And this...

TLW RH KZGRVMG

And this...

TLW RH ULITRERMT

Or this...

TLW RH FMXSZMTRMT

Or even this...

TLW RH GIFHGDLIGSB

And just in case your codecracking skills temporarily failed you, here's the answers...

CREATOR
PERFECT
LOVING
PATIENT
FORGIVING
UNCHANGING
TRUSTWORTHY

Fascinating Fact:

*Did you know that God's mind is so incredible
that the Bible says that if your had a crack at trying
to count up God's thoughts they'd be more than
all the grains of sand on the seashore put together.
And just have a think about how many grains of sand
your average beach holds!
What it means is that you simply can't count
how many thoughts God has - there's just too
many of them!*

Having promised you a shot at getting a picture of God way back at the beginining of this book, now's the time to unveil the finished result.

Okay, so we're not gonna get to see what God actually *looks* like (this side of heaven) but as we've now discovered, the Bible is a pretty good source of info to get yourself a **clear picture** of the *sort* of God he is.

So now that we *know*, what are we gonna *do* about it?

I know, how about we dive into one more quick Bible bit to get ourselves an answer.

Jacob has a bundle with God!

If you've read Boring Bible book *Hotchpotch Hebrews* then you'll know all about a chap called **Jacob**.

(Just for your info, he was the dad of Joseph, the guy with the multi-coloured coat).

Jacob had been through a bit of a rough time over the last few years but to be perfectly honest he only had himself to blame.

In fact he'd had to leave home in a hurry many years earlier 'cos he'd cheated his elder brother (**Esau**) out of his rights as the eldest son.

Let's not beat about the bush, Jacob had gotten himself a bit of a reputation as **a cheat**!

But Jacob had *one* thing in his favour...

JUST ONE?
DON'T GO
OVERBOARD
ON THE PRAISE
WILL YOU!

Jacob was a man who (in his heart of hearts) wanted to please God. Jacob had done a lot of things *his* way through his life but the time had come to change all that.

He was finally heading home (to **Canaan**) to face the consequences of his past mistakes but something needed to change. Jacob now needed to let *God* take control of his life. Jacob needed to start relying on God and not on what *he* could do. And here's how it all changed.

One night, on his journey home, Jacob was approached by a man. Of all the strange things, the man began to wrestle with Jacob. But Jacob gave as good as he got.

Who won the fight?

Jacob.

Who was the man?

The Bible says that it was God.

What was it all in aid of?

God wanted to see how serious Jacob was about needing God to run his life.

You see, Jacob had got to know God over the years and the more he discovered about God the more Jacob realised that he needed God more than ever.

That's why Jacob simply wouldn't let go his grip on God until God blessed him.

This Boring Bible book has given you a bit of a glimpse of what God is like - a sort of **picture of God** like we said at the start. Are you going to be like Jacob and decide that, with the info you've now got of what God is like, you're gonna make him **No.1 in your life**?

Or are you just gonna ignore the fact that there really *is* a God who created everything (including **you**) and who's done *everything* that needs to be done for you to be able to call this awesome God...

And just before we go our separate ways perhaps I ought to tell you that calling God '**The Big Boss**' is probably *not* a very good idea.

After all the things we've discovered about him being a loving **Father**, a faithful **Son** and an awesome **Holy Spirit**, it hardly does God justice, does it?

Until the *next* Boring Bible book (and there's *loads* of 'em)...

See ya!